Dandelions and Defiance

poems by

Chloe Viner

Finishing Line Press
Georgetown, Kentucky

Dandelions and Defiance

Copyright © 2018 by Chloe Viner
ISBN 978-1-63534-780-7 First Edition
All rights reserved under International and Pan-American Copyright Conventions. No part of this book may be reproduced in any manner whatsoever without written permission from the publisher, except in the case of brief quotations embodied in critical articles and reviews.

ACKNOWLEDGMENTS

Some of the poems in *Dandelions and Defiance* have been previously published, "Thelma" was published in *Third Wednesday Literary and Arts Journal*. "Heritage" was also published in *Third Wednesday Literary Arts Journal*.

This book is dedicated to Ashley Hiatt, whose support and friendship means the world to me. Earlier this year I came close to losing her and nothing has ever terrified me more. I am so thankful for her steadfast friendship over the years.

Publisher: Leah Maines
Editor: Christen Kincaid
Cover Art: Chloe Viner
Author Photo: Shane Collins
Cover Design: Leah Huete

Printed in the USA on acid-free paper.
Order online: www.finishinglinepress.com
also available on amazon.com

Author inquiries and mail orders:
Finishing Line Press
P. O. Box 1626
Georgetown, Kentucky 40324
U. S. A.

Table of Contents

Thelma 1

Source Material 2

Beufort 3

Goodbye 4

Heritage 5

Speak 6

Mud Season 7

The Art of Floral Arrangement 8

Herpetology 9

Coping Mechanism 10

Rancher 11

Harvest 12

Residue 13

Games We Play 14

1000 Pieces 16

Swimming 17

Carving 18

Story Telling 19

Bargaining 20

Snake Bite 21

Limbless 22

Built 23

Thelma

Red feathered and fly
trapped in a femur white tower of teeth
wings at awkward angles like
grass growing between sidewalk
feet like her ancestor, T-rex grip
she is seventy-five more moments
of tick-eating sunbathing glory
arches her back and sets loose
a necklace of beads sliding off the chord
all that work, undone,
and the Fox full of her kin
sighs and retires

She hobbles home
I care for her,
warm water, maggot removal, hydrogen peroxide, ointment,
head down, hiding in dark corners,
not reacting to my touch
a toy broken and cast aside
batteries wasted
but today
she perches back in her spot,
squawks holy hell when I try to touch her
no longer complacent under a running faucet
glares at me and pecks at her feed
a concentration survivor who has escaped death's door
she peaks outside, ready almost, to resume
those seventy-five more moments

Source Material

Feathers slide off her wings
letters land in corn fields
vowels dot the petals of sunflowers
consonants float down rapid river bends
words escape her wings
like pings from cell towers and satellite dishes

Beufort

North Pacific Grey whales travel 12,400 miles
from Baja to Beufort sea
each wave that touches them
part of their journey
until the whole ocean bears witness
to their epic saga.

Bees get the bulk of credit but
between 100 and 200 thousand animals pollinate
it's like calling a ballerina the only dancer
tap, classical, and ballroom
carry seeds out doors and through walkways
blooming petals from the tips of
ballet flats, Irish dancing shoes, and flamenco heels

Feathers, waves, and petals spell each journey
until we forgo the familiar alphabet and communicate
with wing beats, migrations and pollinated flowers.

Goodbye

The wail of a mother burying her child
trying to gather the fragments of herself
white rose petals blowing past freshly marked gravesites
they forgot to tell her zoning wouldn't allow a standing gravestone
instead plaque in the ground
feet crossing thresholds
icy rain, snow pelts down on black hats and winter jacket hoods
ash, perfume, roses, burning wicks
line up; drop a rose and a handful of dirt
vibrancy buried, like him.

Priest gives a biblical anecdote,
God taking away a couple's children to test their faith
God.
What a fucking asshole.

We are organ donors
gaping holes,
no doctor to replace what has been taken
waking in a bathtub full of ice
extracted liver, sitting in Walmart cooler
violated, bloody footprints on the floor
out of place in this pristine room
the funeral home owner grim reaper
to finalize what has been taken
painting over cracked wall
thinking the color will cover fissures
no glue, tape, caulk, paint, faith,
just the salt of our tears on our lips.

Heritage

My family, a swimming pool of Schizophrenia
waves of bi-polar, splashes of depression
it's hard to be born here
to emerge from the water
not dripping of these things
to towel off these tendencies
psychosis dripping from my dark locks

I've left the poolside
but I go there often in response to
cries for help
find my brother, mother, aunt,
drowning

There is no line, no floating device,
nothing I toss them ever adheres
I've spent decades
scrambling poolside, grabbing lifesavers and rope

I fear someday I will pull their limp bodies from the water
administer CPR and find no breath left in their corpses
that I will stand at each of their funerals
feeling the futility of a life spent poolside.

Speak

I'm naked,
you circle with shears
lopping off adjectives and ears
slicing moments and fingers
leaving a bloody pool of letters and bones
my body has no value to anyone but me
words buried in the soil with scraps of flesh
tendrils of thoughts and organs poking through the dirt

I will mark this terrain
So that those who walk this way
know I died one thousand deaths
just to speak these words.

Mud Season

Life is sepia colored
Vermont in February
grey browns and dark reds
sap trickling down bark
anxieties exuding from my skin
tires spinning
car battered brown
bottoming out rocks scrape her undercarriage
jagged slices hewn from my stomach and torso
food is flavorless
thoughts have dulled points
not the road less travelled by
I have been here many times before
most blue berries are safe to eat
but nothing bright speckles the landscape
a birdfeeder set out too late in the season
abandoned farmhouses
broken gates
I sit between two oaks and know
the sun will set
and nothing new will rise tomorrow.

The Art of Floral Arrangement

My first memory is my mother pushing my father
down a flight of steep wooden stairs
he lied to me then
I spent all those years waiting for my mother
the way a blind man craves sight
not really sure what it would be like
but knowing it was an essential human experience
she fantasized about killing me
I was willing to die
I didn't start wanting to live until I was twenty
spent the eleven years between dragging my body across
the track
leaving a smudged reminder like a slug leaves a trail.

Herpetology

I am a Sea Turtle
laying two hundred seventy-three eggs
hoping one hatchling will survive
carry my thoughts through the ocean
come back mature
carry on my legacy
the first three to five years
 turtles float in seaweed beds
much like my ideas about mortality and UFO's sit
stagnant
hoping to find nourishment
in the folds of my mind

Coping Mechanism

I learned to walk around land mines as a child
steer clear of this word
seek refuge from that facial expression
duck behind rubble at that tone of voice
when my step faltered
I found myself in need of a tourniquet
bleeding, injuries not tended
I learned crude stitches
elementary ways to wrap cloth around wounds
mechanisms to survive the battle field

Now I'm a soldier who has returned from war,
I duck behind buildings when cars backfire
I wake up in the night screaming
none of these mechanism save me
like a man stumbling
on a phantom limb

I grapple to realize no one is aiming their weapon at me
I have trouble comprehending I am safe
I lay out my bandages, thread and needle,
I travel prepared for injury

When I sense a threat I look for cover
a veteran of abuse
I live in flight
heart never stops racing,
always sure that another landmine
is around the corner.

Rancher

Some days I have to wrangle my desire to kill myself
like a rancher with cattle,
roping off each run away thought
tying knots around stubborn straining necks
thick with muscle from too many years of use
thoughts bucking and writhing
determined to break free
drenched in mud and sweat
straining against barn doors
like Atlas holds the world
relief in the form of continents
out of reach

Replaying my weakness like an old western film
knowing that in the end only one of us will stand, gun raised.

On good days I'm the lone hero, an out-of-towner
riding a horse from auction
on others, the trespasser
standing in dirt roads waiting for gunslingers
to finish me off,
dreaming of sweet relief
in blood and soil.

Harvest

I dreamt that you died last night
the funeral home said I couldn't have a service
 not enough people would come
I told them I had enough love to fill fifty seats
overflow into fifty glasses to toast with

Your illness is the air we breathe
the water we swim in
the food we eat
inextricably entwined

If only I could collect your gifts
a farmer harvesting flint corn
tossing aside the sick ears
like a lemon car that you keep buying spare parts for
I'm always trying to replace the broken bits
or weed them out

If I was Fish and Wildlife Services
I'd cull the problem,
but the beauty would lie in the fallen Bison

there is no sieve
no machine that can separate
if you die
we lose it all.

Residue

If I sorted these moments
by shape, color, smell, texture
chose moments as fabrics
silks, cottons, Parisian wool
filled beds and couches with
afternoons in wildlife refuges,
chickens fluffing speckled feathers in dust baths
rescue mutts running as keys turn

If I made a voodoo doll of moments:
rape, suicide attempt, isolation
unraveled at the seams
burned in the wood pile
until the smell of those traumas
Milwaukee's Best, vomit, gauze, sweat filled sheets
clung to nothing but my hair.

Games We Play

Checkers, Chess, Risk or Monopoly
playing these games since childhood
we've confused the rules
you King me while I checkmate Park Place
If only I could gather the manuals
decipher the rules and regulations

Morse code over a static radio line
before the bombs go off
but I'm always scouting when I should be home
an old man at the beach with his metal detector
tarnished nickels and costume jewelry caked in mud
I convince myself there is
gold at the end of the rainbow
and not another broken tile in the mosaic
of all the times
my love could not save you

You're holding a gun to your head
the chamber changes
from suicide to murder
to a hunger strike in prison
to a drug deal gone bad
to another three years of
plastic chairs in visiting rooms
you've spent as many years inside as outside
which makes sense since you were built
inside out

Chances bubble up on sunny days,
sand castles at the beach
easily swept away by current,
always rebuilding before
greedy waves swallow our progress
I feel guilty for thinking
if the gun fires
I can finally rest
but it's a misnomer
I will never rest
I will always love you as I stand on the shore of
three hundred seventy-five sand castles
and a tide that always comes back.

1000 Pieces

My life is a puzzle
not all of the pieces fit together
some are missing
damaged and malformed
no longer clicking into place
some seem like they go to a completely different puzzle
I spend the years trying to make a complete image
out of something that was never meant to be cohesive

It took me thirty years to realize that pieces don't have to make one landscape
this puzzle doesn't need to be framed in a living room

Now I make the pieces into jewelry,
I use them to pay bills
I sauté them over low heat
I tuck in the corners at night and tell them I love them

I lift a large piece to cover myself from the downpour
and remember when I thought that flimsy cardboard
was a poor legacy
look at me now eating the edges
and blooming from seeds I've planted
in compost and cardboard.

Swimming

I fall into my own cracks and disappear
like those images made up of a thousand dots
I could never quite make out as a kid
standing on the shore of my shortcomings
my feet wet with all these drowned expectations
you told me you would love me always
does that include when I don't love myself
when I've swum a thousand laps
and I'm still treading water
when I've lost my breath and my orientation
and I'm pulling you down just to keep my ahead above wavebreak
when every ounce of us is salt tears
and you've woken to find me cracked and imperfect
will you resent the wreckage?
Or kiss me sweetly in the rain
and begin again?

Carving

I hate people
we used to live between cracks
in the sidewalk
making our way in dandelions and defiance
we've been cemented over now
years of chemicals preventing new growth
that's the way the anti-psychotics treated you
gluing you inside out
I'm still here pressing into the stones around me
trying to make room with chisels of love
in this industrial wasteland
maybe one day we will meet for coffee
in our sixties
I've never pictured you alive that long
and I can tell you that I still spend my Saturdays
carving rocks free of their moorings

Story Telling

If I could take these tears
compound them to make a fine lead
I would use them to write your story
to spell words not in the dictionary
experiences not in the Rockwell repertoire
this young boy at the doctor's office
is not getting his knee reflexes checked
there is no lollipop on the way out
no cute appointment card with
sticky back side to put on your work calendar

You're a puzzle
so much water has been spilled on your pieces
that they flake apart in layers
no longer fit together
mashed cardboard and shredded images
how can we put you together like this?
now I wish I could confine you
that I could put you together like the
strewn pieces of Lego on the playroom floor
build onto you with every attribute
pull out cracked old pieces

A giraffe at the zoo with his 25-pound heart
beating blood up that long neck
I'm here hoping that your mind might be cleared of rust
a rag on a bicycle dipped in vinegar
brown water in a bucket
silver shining handles
if I could refurbish your mind like this
dirt beneath my fingernails
tools in hand
I'd be in the garage now
replacing every broken bit.

Bargaining

I made the plaster for the cast
but this isn't a hospital and those aren't broken bones
I poured the rubbing alcohol
but those wounds got infected anyway
I paced the hallways
watched the phone
talked through Plexiglas
on plastic phones
wore the sports bra so the underwire
wouldn't set off the detector
called lawyers
pleaded with counselors
screamed at God
bargained, begged
too many stages to this grief
I'm always cast on one of them
my wig off kilter
make up too bright
trying desperately to remember the right
lines

Snake Bite

Sometimes I miss slicing my wrists
release of transferring
pain to the outside
those injuries are easy; stitches, bacitracin, band aids
they have yet to design a thread that mends
unspoken words, cruel looks, broken trust
that reassures, that stiches along the line of
self-doubt, self-hate, and loneliness sewing a bridge
between people, places, thoughts.

All the people I have loved are
Russian dolls, stacked together inside me
how do I still feel so empty?
Someone told me once that the common denominator
between all my abusers is me,
sometimes I wake up,
moon beams across my bed
gasping for a breath that is stolen in my dreams
and I wonder if it's true.

Does sucking a snake bite wound really work?
Or will I still die with a wound on my arm and venom on my tongue?

Limbless

When we were toddlers
you would distract me
when our parents fought
another round of hide and seek
in a closet while the worst played out
sitting side by side like we did then
four and six
you would tell me
about dragons

The shouts are yours now
I cannot distract you from the dragon
of your psychosis
I hope that the pieces of you might be preserved
so they may become appendages once more

I'm here holding your hand but there is
no body attached.

Built

A broken clock is right twice a day
but even I fall short of those expectations
I've wrapped myself in cellophane and paper towels
I crinkle and wrinkle every time I move
these moments spelled in paper mache
dipping each in a thick paste of
what you expect and I hope
and realizing flour and water can only hold together so much.

I'm lost on a road I've driven
three hundred times before
I can't pull the words loose
bricked together
mortar and red and every tear I've cried

these walls we've built
these trails we've hiked
these roads we've driven
these years we've spent
nothing can tear down the monuments and walls
we've built
even if it's just flour and water and a little bit of
us.

Chloe Viner is the author of several books of poetry. Her first book, *Naked Under an Umbrella* was published by Finishing Line Press in 2011. Her second book, *What the Rain Said Last Night,* was published in 2015 by Future Cycle Press. Her Third book, *27 Apples*, was published in 2016 by Finishing Line Press. This is her fourth book. Chloe received her Juris Doctor and Master's in Environmental Law and Policy from Vermont Law School in 2012. Chloe works in the field of Restorative Justice as the Panel Manager at Franklin Grand Isle Restorative Justice Center. In her spare time she enjoys hiking, reading, writing, baking, and spending time with her rescued dogs, cat and flock of hens. Chloe and her husband Shane are excitedly awaiting the arrival of their twin boys, Armand and Julian by December 2018.

www.ingramcontent.com/pod-product-compliance
Lightning Source LLC
LaVergne TN
LVHW041521070426
835507LV00012B/1742